Mystical AF

A VERY ARIES JOURNEY FROM
DARKNESS TO LIGHTNESS OF BEING

BY NATALIA BENSON

MYSTICAL AF shares Natalia's journey from darkness to lightness of being, through love, loss, spirituality, self-discovery and ultimately, success. This personal memoir utilizes the lens of Astrology as it guides the reader to uncover their own unique purpose, and shares mystical yet practical tools to help infuse the sacred into your everyday life.

*I wrote this book to encourage and remind
you that you can do anything.*

*This book is dedicated to:
my Mamma & Poppa (Capricorn & Scorpio),
Tarot my pup (a Pisces) & Mick my love (Capricorn).*

And most of all of you. Thank you for being on this journey with me.

Contents

Introduction

Aries Sun, Capricorn Rising with a Sagittarius Moon

*Aries Sun: a natural leader, does not go with the
status quo, remarkably independent
Capricorn Rising: old soul energy, projects oneself as
highly competent and maybe even too serious
Sagittarius Moon: a natural optimist, slightly
flighty, always willing to teach*

My backstory, to me, is perfect. Whether or not you are familiar with who I am, through my Instagram, podcast or courses, I have faith that you'll be able to cultivate a connection to my journey while noticing your own remarkable ability to extract peace and spiritual growth from any experience in your life. Perhaps you will even come to call your own past perfect, too.

I base each chapter on an aspect of my Natal Chart because amazingly enough, Astrology is what changed and perhaps even saved my life. If you aren't totally clear on what the Aspects or Astrology jargon mean, do not worry! Follow along as best you can and I am positive by the end of this book you will understand a little bit more about Astrology simply by reading my story. Astrology at its core is like a spiritual psychology - a cosmic study of human behavior and expression. It's a language, and once you learn a few simple phrases, a lot of magic can unfold in your life!

At the beginning of each Chapter I give a small interpretation of the placement in my Natal Chart that gave rise to the lesson presented in each storyline. This interpretation is based on my 10+ years of studying and getting to know Astrology and my Natal Birth Chart. A Natal Chart by the way, is an Astrological Chart based on the time, place & date of your birth. It's basically a snapshot of what was happening in the heavens the moment you were born.

It is also helpful to note that the timeline of this book tends to shift and jump around a bit, as I express and explore what a powerful, challenging and mystical journey my twenties and early life were.

Lastly, I do want to thank you for going on this ride with me. At the end of each chapter, I will offer a little Life Lesson & a Mystical AF Soul Tip to encapsulate what that particular phase of life taught me and how you can bring a little (or a lot!) more magic into your life. I pray you can carry these little tidbits with you into your own everyday experience and enrich your life with more self awareness and peace.

So you're here, let's begin.

Life Lesson: You can do anything if you're willing to trust yourself, love yourself and honor the process of becoming who you are truly meant to be. It may not be easy, but I guarantee that it will be worth it.

One

Venus in Pisces

A Broken Heart & My Spiritual Awakening

Venus in Pisces: an exaltation in Astrology, but tends to show itself as an aspect that allows one to feel way too much and give way too much, often times to those who have never proven they deserve it. Pisces can express itself as escapism from the harshness of the world via drugs, alcohol and/or lovers. In a more healthfully expressed format, Pisces leans towards spirituality, empathy, kindness and creativity, but the shadow side must be faced and integrated before the creative faculties can be explored.

I am not sure when, where or how I realized this, but around the age of 18, I knew that I was just plain sad. I began noticing how much of the world felt so alien and intense for me. When I moved to San Diego from Arizona for college, it was the first time in my life being totally alone. I was always extremely close to my parents, especially my mom. At school, I got to experience the feeling of solitude and I can't say that I liked it very much. It is so hard for human beings to be truly alone. I can acknowledge that from where I sit now it's a much more enjoyable experience, but that is because I feel aligned with my purpose and more actualized as a human being. Yet it's still something I struggle with - being totally alone. In our aloneness we can find the Universe, and it wasn't until I surrendered everything through my struggles and solitude that this relationship to something bigger than my fear began to develop.

During my spiritual evolution, I first turned to relationships with men as my drug of choice. Later it became actual drugs, in an attempt to heal from the sadness I inflicted upon myself in those relationships.

There was one particular relationship with an Aquarius when I was just 19 that I attribute to my spiritual wake-up call. One night, laying in my college apartment, I was about to say my prayers before falling asleep. As a note, I was raised with a very open viewpoint to spirituality and religion. My mom let me explore whatever I wanted, which I fully contribute to my ability to imbibe new-age thought and mindset principles. Still, for whatever reason, I always tended towards a Judeo-Christian way of praying just because that was all I ever really knew. I opened my mouth and uttered a prayer: Dear God... and before I could even finish I realized, Um, wait.... hmmm... wow. Oh shit........ I don't.... I don't even believe in God.

I noticed the room become extremely quiet, and I felt the most alone I ever had before. I thought, Shit...I'm only 19. What is the rest of my life going to look, feel and BE like without some connection to "God?" Fuck... this is going to be interesting.... and then I fell into a deep, dreamless sleep.

Fast forward a few weeks later to meeting Kev, that Aquarius. Little did I know that God (or the Universe, whatever name you relate to best) would answer my questions in the form of a successful, handsome, sandy blonde-haired heartthrob who lived near the beach in an incredible little cottage. It was perfect kryptonite, and sparked an 11 year journey of waking the fuck up to my power. Good thing I didn't know the healing process was going to kick off with such a bang and last for such a long time!!! I now understand that when we want something in life, we will receive a lot of powerful tests that can feel like deterrents, but ultimately are pointing us to exactly what we desire. (It may take some time and a remarkable amount of faith, but this is the way it works, trust me!)

I'd have to say Kev was the first experience of my deep Venus in Pisces wounds, and the feelings of intense abandonment that laid dormant under the surface my entire life. He showed up as an energetic embodiment to help me start to heal myself. Our romance was swift and full on, as any Aries will tell you. I was so young, vulnerable and unaware that I let myself get completely overtaken by this powerful force of a human being. When he and I first started dating, I had been conscious of spirituality for some time, but it wasn't an integral part of my life. The semester prior I had been sick with mono (the kissing and drinking disease, don't ya know...) and taught myself meditation to pass the time when I couldn't go to class or out partying with my friends...

Kev was super spiritual and creative, two things that I didn't really see myself as. I was a Political Science Major at the time and had stopped dancing (my only creative outlet) a few years earlier after leaving High School. Kev represented an energy of something I believed I was not, but deeply ached to experience in my life. At first I wanted to possess him, but later learned that what I truly wanted was to embody that kind of power, spirit and creativity within myself.

A few weeks into Kev and I seeing each other, (which for me was already wrought with pain, fear of abandonment and intense emotional anxiety...) I mentioned I was interested in learning more about spirituality. He proceeded to hand me two books that would kick start my journey home to myself - Conversations with God by Neale Donald Walsh and The Celestine Prophecy by James Redfield. While both were instrumental in my awakening, reading Conversations with God absolutely changed my life.

On my way home from Kev's the next morning, I decided to stop at Balboa Park and visit the Annie Leibovitz exhibition. If you've never been, Balboa Park is majestic and stunningly beautiful. Surrounded by massive trees and tons of greenery, it's one of my favorite places in the world (and ironically where I received my first intuitive reading, before I ever saw myself as "spiritual".) As I sat in my car waiting to go into the exhibit, something prompted me to grab the book off my seat and read the back cover. It said:

"Suppose you could ask God the most puzzling questions about existence - questions about love and faith, life and death, good and evil. Suppose God provided clear, understandable answers. It happened to Neale Donald Walsch. It can happen to you. You are about to have a conversation... I have heard the crying of your heart. I have seen the searching of your soul. I know how deeply you have desired the Truth. In pain have you called out for it, and in joy. Unendingly have you beseeched Me. Show Myself. Explain Myself. Reveal Myself. I am doing so here, in terms so plain, you cannot misunderstand. In language so simple, you cannot be confused. In vocabulary so common, you cannot get lost in the verbiage. So go ahead now. Ask Me anything. Anything. I will contrive to bring you the answer. The whole universe will I use to do this. So be on the lookout; this book is far from My only tool. You may ask a question, then put this book down. But watch.

Listen. The words to the next song you hear. The information in the next article you read. The storyline of the next movie you watch. The chance utterance of the next person you meet. Or the whisper of the next river, the next ocean, the next breeze that caresses your ear - all these devices are Mine; all these avenues are open to Me. I will speak to you if you will listen. I will come to you if you will invite Me. I will show you then that I have always been there. All ways."

It was the first time in my life where I cried out of sheer relief. As if something in the Universe was finally responding to me, telling me I didn't have to live life alone. I cried because I realized we are seen, we are acknowledged, and we are One with God's Universe.

Now looking back on it, I realize that the Universe had always heard me, and answered all my questions in a very roundabout way. At the time, it was initially through a handsome man who lived by the beach, with great taste in spiritual books! And soon, what would seem like a string of heartbreaks, would really be the path towards a greater understanding of my Soul's mission.

Kev eventually broke up with me by not texting or calling me for nearly three weeks. I am not sure I had ever experienced so much physical pain from emotional torment before. I am also not sure why I didn't simply call and ask what was going on - I suppose I hadn't found my voice yet. He later began dating the woman who introduced us. Ironically, I had dreams about that repeatedly, but didn't receive true confirmation until she emailed me two months later to clear the air and tell me they were together. Ouch.

Right before receiving that message and in the intensity of those weeks of silence, I started my first creative endeavor and my first business: a jewelry line that I would continue to work on and build for nearly 9 years. I birthed something beautiful and empowering out of deep disappointment; this was the true lesson. I inevitably changed my major to Art, leaving behind Political Science and the idea that I was going to change the world from the outside. I realized the world will shift and heal from each individual deciding to love and nourish themselves on the inside, first. Imagine seven billion people who love and value themselves, and how beautifully they would show up in the world! I've based all of my work and purpose off of this basic principle that I received when I was 19 years old. Getting broken up with by a dude living by the beach became the perfect catalyst for me to jump start my entire soul's mission. When one door closes, one million more open. Thanks, Kev. (But really, thanks Universe & thank you, Me.)

Life Lesson: The Universe responds to us. Ask the question and you will be answered. Don't be surprised if it's in a way you never could have imagined. Stay open, you will be responded to.

Mystical AF Soul Tip: Read the book Conversations with God by Neale Donald Walsch. To see ALL of my favorite spiritual book recommendations go to: nataliabenson.com/mysticalAF or stay tuned for the final chapter of this book.

Two

North Node in Aries

Discovering My True North via The Tarot

North Node in Aries: The North Node in Astrology is your soul's greatest trajectory in a lifetime, but it will feel very foreign and challenging when you first begin to pursue it. Aries is the sign of the leader, the individual, one who is very self-motivated.

I think there's something within all of us that really, really wants to know why we are here.

When I was younger and living in Ahwatukee, Arizona, I remember walking alone in my neighborhood at night near the South Mountain Range. I absolutely loved my neighborhood and felt so safe, comfortable and held there. Each night I would look up at the stars, enchanted by their delicate glow. I've always had a warmth in my heart for moments that most people don't often pay attention to.

I remember one particular night I was connecting with the stars above me and I said out loud, *I am really going to be something… I know I am here to live a big life… I don't know how I know it… I just know it…*

I felt so held by my visions, and a deep, innocent view of my future at the age of 18. I still remember this moment as one of the first times

I was able to hear my soul speaking through me, and me actually being willing to listen.

There is something powerful in understanding the North Node of one's natal chart. The North Node is all about the True Node of one's Soul, so to speak. Mine happens to be placed in Aries, along with three other powerful planets: My Sun, Mercury and Jupiter. I learned about the North Node as the soul's calling for our progress and evolution when I was 22 years old, receiving my first ever natal chart reading from Southern California Astrologer, Christopher Witecki. This name will forever be imprinted in my mind and heart as someone who really helped me develop myself spiritually and realize my esoteric potential at such a young age.

Christopher created a space called SoulGarden.tv that I studied and subscribed to religiously. We didn't call it "content" back then, and there was no Instagram yet. He produced Astrology videos and educational materials, daily! He also empowered other healers and teachers with a platform to do the same.

I had absolutely no money at this time. I was a jewelry designer and still in school, because my parents begged me to get a college degree. I could barely afford the $10 monthly subscription but I knew it was important, so I kept with my mini-investment and settled for eating scrambled eggs, a lot. I was struggling with a major cocaine addiction because I still felt so lost, sensitive and hungry for authentic connection. I would go out and party, sometimes coming home with heart palpitations from bad cocaine and too much alcohol. Still, I would turn on SoulGarden and watch. I did so much spiritual study in the throes of the Los Angeles party scene, seeking wisdom, guidance, truth and solace in something that felt deeper and bigger than what I was experiencing at that time. It was honestly the only thing that kept me going and I remember waking up some mornings questioning why I was even alive. Amidst all of the pain, I just kept watching SoulGarden, and tuning into Christopher Witecki. I continued to learn Astrology and read Spiritual Books, I kept doing my best to learn tools that would help me feel more whole and less alone. I even began going to classes on Tuesday evenings at a woman named Irene's home. She was teaching women how to tap into their inner wisdom through basic shamanic practices. What other 23 year old was there with me? Just me, and attending these classes filled me with so much joy and hope, that life could actually get better.

On SoulGarden, Christopher and his team created videos filled with everything from essential oils, past life regression, to crystal wisdom, astrology and tarot.... Tarot. People ask me all the time how I started working with the Tarot. Were my parent's mystical practitioners, or, uber spiritual? Well, my dad is a retired CFO and my mom worked in the Pharmaceutical industry, so no, I definitely didn't learn the Tarot from them.

I remember seeing a woman on Christopher's channel teaching about the Death card and explaining the energy behind the Tarot. I was captivated, and knew I wanted to study this work in a bigger way. It was in this moment that I said to myself, *Hey Universe, I am ready to become a student of the Tarot, so I am trusting in you to bring me my teacher whenever the moment is right...* Fast forward to one beautiful sunny afternoon in Laguna Beach, California at my Aries friend Rudy's place. Her mom Diane, also an Aries, always felt like a soulmate to me, even though there was geographic distance and many years between us. I noticed on Diane's bedside table that we were reading the same book - Love, Freedom, Aloneness by Osho.

I have a theory. If you truly ask the Universe something, from the deepest spaces of your heart, in a state of awe and surrender, you will get an answer. The Universe always answers us, but when we are asking the big picture, soul-shifting Dharmic stuff, I truly believe that answer often arrives instantaneously. I picked up our matching book and underneath it was yet another book, but this time, it was the one that would shape the basis of my esoteric unfolding - Tarot: Mirror of the Soul by Gerd Ziegler. It hit me instantly, YES! Diane is going to teach me the Tarot!

At the time, I was in yet another emotionally debilitating relationship. Only this guy, a Leo from Orange County, wouldn't even remotely commit to me, flirted with other girls in front of my face, and was a terrible alcoholic. I asked Diane to give me my first Tarot reading ever and consider teaching me the system of the Tarot. Still feeling so broken hearted, abandoned and lost I felt like learning the Tarot was something that was just next in my spiritual unfolding. I felt like understanding the Tarot could help me nourish and fill myself up, instead of looking for young guys and the "security" of a relationship to validate my existence and help me feel safe.

My first Tarot session with Diane felt like I was finally giving my thirsty soul a drink of water; it felt like the nourishment and assurance that only clear loving truths can provide. I learned that when we forget about our spirit and live only in the mind and body, our soul cries out for attention through feelings of sadness, emotional starvation and pain. I know that might sound intense, but until we finally realize that we are tri-part beings (mind, body and soul), we suffer and often look for outside means of validation and fulfillment. Diane reminded me of all of this in my first Tarot reading ever. I don't remember exactly what she said - she reminded me about the power within myself and gave me soulful insights around my current Leo "relationship". I remember she pulled The Star card, and printed some pages of information for me from the book. I read every single word, line and prompt, as if my life depended on it. At the time, I truly needed the wisdom and hope I found on those pages and within that reading. I needed someone to tell me that everything in my life was going to be ok.

Still, Diane never really agreed to teach me the Tarot. A few weeks later, I received a package in the mail. Wrapped in one of Diane's paintings was the Gerd Ziegler Book, Tarot: Mirror of the Soul and a deck of Thoth Tarot Cards with a hand-painted message: "The Journey is Sublime."

The journey is sublime.

How beautiful. Even when we aren't paying attention, our life path is always unfolding before us. Learning the Tarot and delving into my ability to make deeper sense of my problems was such a saving grace for me. I always say that the Mystical saved my life. I became obsessed with studying the cards and even helping the people around me find answers to their own personal questions through readings. As soon as I felt even remotely confident I started offering Tarot sessions at events and pulling cards for anyone who was remotely interested! I kept the book Diane had sent me close at hand to help guide my intuition and serve the inner peace of those I read for, I didn't have any qualms about being seen as a beginner reader, I just wanted to help and get started as quickly as possible. I knew that an important leg of my journey had begun. I started feeling a little more light, a little more together, a little more whole, with or without a boyfriend or someone to date. I eventually completed that "relationship" with the Leo, realizing that my heart and soul deserved so much more. I slowly began to heed the messages from The Star Card: "Stay true to yourself & let your star rise."

Life Lesson: You are never lost. Your most incredible life purpose may be found in your deepest confusions. Pay attention to the things that capture your heart and ask the Universe for guidance and clarity, especially if you're not sure where to start.

Mystical AF Soul Tip: Want to study and begin your own journey with the Tarot? First, choose a deck that speaks to you! There is no singular deck to learn from, what is most important is to choose a deck that inspires your heart. Second, find an excellent guidebook that goes along with that deck. (My personal favorite is the Thoth Deck and the guidebook, Tarot: Mirror of the Soul by Gerd Ziegler.) Always make sure the deck you are choosing has empowering messages that encourage you to stay in the driver's seat of your life! Lastly, create a daily practice by choosing a card for yourself every morning or evening and then journaling your findings. This is how I learned the Tarot!

Three

Chiron Conjunct Mars

Spiritual Enlightenment & Boys Being Mean To Me

Chiron Conjunct Mars in the 5th House: Challenge and healing for the sake of spiritual enlightenment, especially with regards to masculine energy, or men in general. Deep desire to heal, shift and transmute one's pain for the sake of empowerment, joy, pleasure and purpose.

When I was young, probably starting around the age of 12 or 13, I got picked on, heavily, by the boys at my school. I was always a unique looking being compared to the people I grew up with in Phoenix, Arizona. My mom's background is Ukrainian and Jewish, my dad's German, Swedish and English. I had a very oval face and angular look, light brown hair and almond-shaped eyes. I had a deep love of horses and was an avid rider in our Equestrian neighborhood. I mention this because ironically, that was what I was tormented with. Boys would tease me and tell me that I looked like a horse. I never knew when a verbal attack was going to come my way. I loved to dress expressively (Venus in Pisces in the 2nd House, thank you very much...) but often found myself dressing to fit in, instead of representing my bright, bubbly spirit. Every time I was on the other side of an insult or horse "nayyyyy" echoing across the school campus, my heart broke and my spirit hid a bit more.

The aspect I am speaking about in my chart is all about healing and coming toward a spiritual understanding around masculine energy. If that sounds like another language to you, let me explain. Chiron is an icy asteroid orbiting the Sun between the planets Saturn and Uranus. Some have even said it could be considered a "dwarf planet" because of its size and constancy in our Solar System. According to Astrologers, Chiron is what's known as The Wounded Healer, and it has a major impact on us energetically. Wherever it shows up in our Natal Chart is where we are meant to deeply heal, evolve and even suffer at times, for the sake of authentic spiritual growth. In Chiron's highest expression, wherever he occupies our chart is where we may be called to help ease other's suffering. As an Astrologer I also like to look at Chiron as a window to a past life experience, where we have been hurt in other incarnations and what we may be bringing emotionally to this present incarnation to heal.

The truth is, right before all of this verbal bullying began, I was getting a little bit full of myself. One thing I have always found fascinating is my deep level of self-awareness. In 6th grade I had a lot of girlfriends and amassed a bit of social popularity at my school. As I transitioned into 7th grade, puberty hit and my face began to elongate and change. As strange as it may sound, when I started getting picked on, it broke my spirit, but it humbled me. Not because I felt I deserved to be humbled, but because I realized how much it hurt to have people be unkind to me. It inspired me to be kind in return, and become a soft space where people felt safe to land. Even though I was so young, I really believe this is where some basic tenants of my personality began.

It no longer meant very much to just be pretty or popular without the energy of kindness, respect and love towards the people around me. I remember during this time, I also began to hear my intuition speak to me. On the way home from school after a verbal attack or a mean encounter during a lunch break, I heard a voice whispering wisdom to me and reminding me of the truth: that I was loved, that they were hurting, and that people who cause others pain are in pain themselves. I was so young but I heard this higher wisdom of intuition quelling my heart. I am sure you know what I am referring to…and if you don't, I trust that because you are reading this book, you will soon.

So hence Chiron's Lesson to the young Natalia Benson: "Through boys (represented as Mars/masculine energy in Astrology) being unkind to you, you will learn humility and the softness to treat others with gentleness and warmth so they don't experience the same pain as you, or at least, not at your hand. You will not amass power or prestige over others at their expense. You will lead from your heart and throughout your life, humility and guidance toward spiritual understanding will likely be experienced through heartache or pain when you are not obeying this karmic lesson."

Alright, karma! Thank you!

And a word about karma, by the way. Karma is not, "you did something bad, you get something bad in return!" Karma is about neutralizing energy. We must first learn through experience how to conduct ourselves, and if we do something towards another that does not come authentically from our heart, we can expect to amass some sort of karmic lesson from that experience. Neutralizing karma is when we choose the higher road. That is how we know we are evolving and leaning towards our higher self, and therefore, towards deeper inner peace. I mention all of this because in my opinion, these are all of Chiron's themes.

So what does Chiron mean for you? As I mentioned, I also believe that Chiron can point to our past lives and the wounds we have brought with us from those incarnations. When I was younger, one of the most vivid dreams I can still remember was that of my parents leaving me somewhere. I woke up weeping. Do you ever wonder about the things that seem to be constant issues in your life? Perpetual worries, fears, anxieties? Well from the mind and heart of a Mystic, I see these things as part of our greatest growth, and our soul's journey forward to inner peace, service and authentic greatness. Without the things that challenge us lifetime to lifetime, we would just breeze through without the need to evolve and learn, which is ultimately the goal of the soul! (That's a cute rhyme, right?)

Study where Chiron is in your natal chart, the house placement and sign. This can give you a powerful view of where your soul most wants to grow and heal in this lifetime, and perhaps where you are meant to serve others. The beautiful thing about Astrology is that once you get flowing with your studies, you will find it's full of things you've already known on a really deep, proverbial level. It will only be shocking because you'll wonder how the heck it all makes so much sense. ;)

Lastly, forgiveness is the healing balm of Chiron. This means forgiveness of others and most of all, forgiveness of self. Each time a resentment arises within me or I find myself making up a story about life, my past or being a "victim," I immediately stop and say, I forgive you. And I am not just forgiving whoever hurt me, I am forgiving myself, too. Being human is not so easy, and we all have moments of crying out, "WHY THE FUCK AM I HERE ANYWAY??!!!!"

Still, *I forgive you*, I say to myself, my soul, and All that is. I know I chose to be here, to flourish, to sometimes hurt, to grow, heal, evolve and teach, for a reason.

Life Lesson: The people who often hurt you the most are the ones who teach you the deepest lessons and remind you why your soul came Here (to Planet Earth). When you can take that pain, neutralize it and turn it into gold, you are doing exactly what your soul wants you to do. You are growing, evolving, learning and serving in a way that is beautifully unique to you.

Mystical AF Soul Tip: Want to figure out where your Chiron is? Go to nataliabenson.com/mysticalAF and click on the Find Your Chiron button. There you'll find a step by step guide on pulling up your Natal Chart and spotting Chiron and the other planets in your chart. I also suggest you take my Free Navigating Your Natal Chart Class if you'd like to get started or even deepen your understanding of Natal Chart Astrology, which is everything I am referring to in this Chapter. Astrology is such a profound way to unlock new information about yourself and your mission, so have fun with this incredible tool!

20

Four

Moon in Sagittarius:
Finding Myself, A Teacher

Moon in Sagittarius: a propensity towards optimism and self-expression, unwaveringly joyous and feels a deep yearning to express the truth at all costs.

Around the age of 24 after finishing school, I was searching for ways to create a livelihood that didn't feel like I was selling my soul. Also wonderful to note, that for the first time since high school, I was in a relationship with someone who actually cared about me; another Leo, who lived in Newport Beach. I first worked at a raw juice bar in Hollywood for a number of years, making about $10 an hour. Still, I loved it, because when I was there I could eat organic food, study my spiritual books and speak with heart-centered, like-minded people. As a means to make rent, I was selling my jewelry through Facebook posts, doing small in person sales as often as possible and taking as many shifts as I could at this little juice bar. Even though I was struggling, I still knew I was in the right place. I even met Skrillex and Fred Durst while I worked there, among other juice-obsessed celebrities because at the time, juice cleansing was the thing to do in Los Angeles.

I am not completely sure how I survived financially, because as I mentioned earlier, paying for even a $10 monthly subscription to my favorite spiritual website was quite the issue for me! I was making money selling jewelry but it was just enough to cover the rent of my Hollywood apartment and I was able to eat thanks to the 50% off discount at the juice bar. I sat one morning at my little kitchen table in my Hollywood apartment (which was just up the street from the juice bar that I worked at), feeling a bit low and depressed, wondering how I would make rent the following month. As I looked up from my chair, I happened to notice a quote I had taped to the wall: "Learning is finding out what you already know. Doing is demonstrating that you know it. Teaching is reminding others that they know just as well as you." (Richard Bach)

And then it hit me. Oh, I'm supposed to teach!

But teach what?!

Well, I thought, I'm a jewelry designer, I know how to make jewelry. And I am super into spirituality, maybe I can teach about one of those things? If you are with me as a student, client or a part of my Instagram Universe now, you may be laughing because yes, this was one of the original moments where my soul realized it was time to put my natal chart to work! It was time to take action and stop being scared of my truest purpose! As I said before, our path and purpose so often unfold almost undetected right under our noses.

I remembered what Christopher Witecki told me in my first Natal Chart reading. He said that I was here with a message to share. It's funny because the first time I ever heard the term "messenger soul," in a random spiritual blog post I felt a super warm feeling in my heart and chest, like "oh yes, this feels so familiar and right to me!!" When

Christopher told me, "you are a messenger soul", I literally screamed. I already knew that in my heart.

Even amidst my inner "Yes," so much insecurity welled up within me as I pondered what it would be like to teach my first class. How would I do it? And would anyone even come? Would I be embarrassed because I failed? Will everyone think of me as a failure?! But the feeling of excitement, that same warmth within my chest and tummy reminded me: "Yes babe, this is the way forward." Not to mention, having to figure out how to pay my rent was an excellent incentive to actually just go for it. I decided to stop playing small and start sharing my gifts. So I made flyers and promoted my classes through Facebook, word of mouth and a tiny email list that I usually used to announce sales for my jewelry line.

I first taught a jewelry-making workshop in my apartment and about 10 women showed up. That was one of my first experiences monetizing my skills and receiving payment through my ingenuity with social media marketing. I felt accomplished and deeply fulfilled for the first time in my entire life. I loved the feeling of teaching other women something that brought me not only a livelihood (even if it was a small one!) but helped me feel like I had an identity and a craft. The next class I taught was on sacred sexuality and this is where shit gets interesting.

You might be asking yourself, who was I to teach sacred sexuality? I was recently healing from a cocaine addiction (at that point I was about one year out and just beginning to tap into my deep spiritual reserves with Kundalini Yoga, Meditation and other modalities) and if you have ever been someone who has partied you know there isn't much sacred about a fear of intimacy and only hooking up with people when you're high. The truth is that throughout my years of partying, I barely had sex at all. I was so afraid of being abandoned, hurt and rejected that

I exchanged the frightening unknowns I attributed to true intimacy and close relationships for the high of drugs and alcohol. My boyfriend at the time was the first person I had been with in years who had any vested interested in the health of my heart, my body and my spirit, and it took me a long time to trust that I was safe and could let my guard down.

So remember in the last chapter how I talked a bit about Chiron, hurts and past life energy? I believe there are certain things we just know beyond a shadow of a doubt and it's beyond logic how we actually know it. Perhaps stuff we bring with us from other lifetimes to share and explore in our present incarnation.

Well, for me that stuff was sacred sexuality. There was this wisdom within me that knew there is energy present in sex, and so much healing that can be done through conscious sexual exchange.

Now, let's be clear. It's not like I was practicing that with my then 25 year old boyfriend. When I told him once on a road trip home to Arizona that I was teaching a class on sacred sexuality, he paused a moment and looked in my direction, "Who, you??" It was kind of a hilarious moment because I realized, Wow, I know things deep within my heart and my soul that I don't seem to have the confidence to practice yet… It was also quite weird that I would be teaching a class to about 24 people on sacred sexuality: what it was, how to heal with it as well as letting people ask me deep questions on the subject that I truly knew the answers to… and yet, I still had deep intimacy issues myself. I remember in that class I guided this group through a visualization into their own subconscious on who they needed to apologize to from their past. Perhaps someone who had hurt their sense of dignity or their relationship to their own sense of sacred sensual expression. People were weeping, I was weeping. And I kept asking myself, how the fuck am I doing this? Where is this coming from? But I knew exactly what I was doing and I knew exactly where it was coming from: my heart. Until that time I hadn't really admitted to myself that my whole stint with drugs and alcohol and total avoidance of intimacy was stemming from what happened to me when I was about 6 or 7 - when a 40-something-year-old man made me touch his genitals. That single, one-time occurrence destroyed my sense of trust in men, and it wasn't until I found Kundalini Yoga and the deep spiritual work of my early twenties that I began to heal my heart and my relationship to sex and intimacy. Teaching, sharing and claiming my perennial identity through spirituality and in this case, teaching sacred sexuality, helped me heal. And as I taught this deep meditation where everyone went down into their own hearts and forgave someone who had betrayed them, I finally decided to forgive him.

I think this also goes to show that to teach, you do not have to be perfect. Just earnestly connected to your path and your willingness to heal and grow, so you can help guide others on their path to healing and growing, too.

This is the power in trusting who we are, even when we don't have all the evidence yet. This is how I began my entire career. I trusted the space of my heart and trusted that as long as I was keeping up with my studies, my inner work, channeling information from my heart and remaining in my integrity towards service and liberation, that I was on the perfect path for my highest unfoldment and hey, it turns out that I was right.

My Moon in Sagittarius' placement is the energy of the storyteller, the teacher, the seer, and the truth sharer. But here is the thing, oftentimes the Moon reveals what is hidden in our personalities. See how in this example it was almost hidden to me, this deep wealth of wisdom that was dying to be shared in my life, my work and even my relationships? I just had to accept this deep yearning within me and begin to take action on following my heart. I had to trust that what I had to share was relevant and important. And that in helping others to heal their stories, I could heal mine, too.

I wish I could tell you that everything just took off from there. It definitely didn't. I remember seeing a cartoon about the difference between what success is thought to look like and what it actually looks like, illustrated through a drawing of lines. The first line represents what success is thought to look like, and is a straight arrow heading to the proverbial top unscathed! The second line demonstrates what success actually looks like, and reveals about 200+ crazy, squiggly lines in all directions before FINALLY making its way to the top. An incredible reminder that the journey to the ultimate expression of who we are is windy and it's meant to be that way! I'll next reveal to you how I began to finally hone in on my inner power that paved the way for my teachings and work to express itself as it does today.

Life Lesson: Whatever you tell yourself you are, you are. Whatever title you give yourself, that is your title. Whatever you deeply desire to experience in your life can be true for you, if only you will take the risks, take the leap and listen to that warmth in your chest even when you're scared out of your mind to do so.

Mystical AF Soul Tip: When it comes to soul purpose, teaching or putting ourselves out there- the whole subject can be truly daunting. Don't think about monetization or longevity too early, focus instead on how you want to feel and how you want to make others feel. Pair it down to feelings and excitements versus over seeding with logistics. Write down a big vision you have for your life, super charge it with a crystal or plant it in a plant box. Then surrender it and let it go to the Universe. Trust that in perfect timing your vision, or that which is most aligned to you, will unfold with ease. Have faith in your own process.

28

Five

Ascendant in Capricorn

Pathways to Power

Ascendant in Capricorn: The placement of the ascendant is discovered when you know your exact time of birth. According to Astrology, it's the personality you emit in public and when you are just getting to know people. It can also denote the energy of your Soul's personality. When the Ascendant is in Capricorn, it can give off an air of authority, act a little too serious or studious and cares deeply about what others think. There's also an unstoppable desire to get to the proverbial top of the mountain, deep soul wisdom that's amassed from many lifetimes, and the seeking of power and empowerment through wisdom and vocation.

Okay, I have a very cool story to share. One that I hope will assist you in believing that there is truly no death, that all energy is connected, and again, when we ask a question of the greater Universe, the Infinite Intelligence, and even our own ancestors, we will get an answer.

As I mentioned, I started my first business at the age of 19. I cannot say this business was born out of love and passion, but instead, out of sheer terror. I remember my dad called me on the phone one day (he's a Scorpio - very mindful around the details of everything, especially our family finances) and he started lecturing me about money. While I cannot remember the exact details, I can remember how it made me feel: panicked, frightened, like my shoulders had been set on fire, and stressed the fuck out. I imagine he told me to be more mindful, or to figure something out so we wouldn't have to pay the exorbitant cost of an Arizona resident attending a California school. Either way, the anxiety that I felt that particular Saturday evening would inevitably change the trajectory of my life.

As soon as we hung up the phone, I made an immediate decision within my head and my heart. I truly believe the best decisions in life are made when we can get those two powerful systems on the same wavelength! I said to myself, "You know, I am done being at the whim of someone else's fears around money. I am going to make my own freakin' money. I am going to have my own source of security outside of my parents. I am OVER THIS."

And on I went. From there, I started my first "business," my first brand. I began crafting jewelry in my bedroom out of a bag of leather that a friend gave me. I sat at my little college desk, sometimes covered with school papers and assignments, and littered it with jewelry tools, scraps of leather and tiny pieces of wire that are most likely still in the carpet nooks of that San Diego apartment!

In typical Capricorn Rising meets Sun in Aries fashion, there was something about having my own business that felt both exhilarating and liberating. My plan? To get n.om (that was its name, pronounced: "gnome") rolling so fervently that I could live off of it when I graduated college, and not have to succumb to my parents' yearnings that I get a "real" job. I decided I would be my OWN boss. I would have my OWN money coming in, and wouldn't be dependent on ANYBODY. And I did just that. While I was in school, I began selling my jewelry to local San Diego boutiques, either on consignment or through direct sales. I loved fielding emails while sitting in class, hearing from a boutique or stylist who wanted to place an order with me. I started selling at local art fairs, tiny trade shows, etc. I also decided to become a stylist myself, so on the side I designed shows and shoots taking place in San Diego, and sometimes even Los Angeles. The lesson here is that whatever you say you are, you are. Much of this enterprise was inspired by that Aquarian who broke my soul open when he ghosted me, and whatever my dad's pressure was on me at that time.

(Also a note: when it comes to family, at the end of the day, I truly believe it's only the love that counts - not necessarily the details. The petty shit around money and fear fades away and love is all that remains. My dad is now one of my biggest fans and throughout my journey, we have learned and grown so much together. Forgive your parents for their fears or projections around you, whatever phase of life you are in, they are doing the best they can with whatever they believe to be true about life!)

You could certainly say I was driven, maybe even a little obsessive, because I was so afraid of failing. I also didn't have a spiritual practice when I lived in San Diego, beginning my first enterprise. If there is one thing over the 10 million things I have learned being a creative entre- preneur, it's that having a relationship to the deepest part of who you are (your soul) is the greatest prerequisite to having a successful busi- ness. Your soul and your relationship to yourself is what will carry you through the tough times. Let's think of building a business - any kind of business, like climbing up a steep mountain when it's raining. You better put your poncho on and take it one step at a time so you can learn the laws of the land while you climb! And don't forget to bring some snacks so you don't starve to death!! As you continue on your journey and go a little higher up the winding path of the proverbial mountain, the view gets better and your breathing regulates. It may not get any easier but at least now you know what it takes to keep climbing.

Still, in the words of Gabby Bernstein, the Universe has your back! Sometime at the beginning of n.om, I was back home in Arizona for a visit to see my family. I recall a key moment driving alone past my old high school. I started to speak out loud to my Grandpa Mitch. Before I share, I want to give you a little backstory on my Grandpa and why this moment was so profound for me.

He passed away when I was about 15 years old, and was the first person I had ever seen dead and lifeless. He left us pretty quickly upon selling his massive electrical contracting business and discovering that he had cancer. It was heartbreaking on every level because it was one of those deaths that we weren't ready for, and it happened so quickly. Even when you have the warning, you can never fully prepare for the magnitude of death.

Growing up I was very close to my Grandpa Mitch. Born to immigrant parents in Detroit, Michigan, his father (my great grandpa) died when he was young and left him with five other brothers and his mother, completely poor. As my mom recalls, he was incredibly enterprising and entrepreneurial from a very young age, selling newspapers on the streets of Detroit shouting taglines like, "Baby Born with Double Head!" to sell more newspapers than his competitors. (Ok, Grandpa that's something we now call clickbait, but way to be ahead of your time!!) There were moments in his youth when his family was so poor that his mom would bake potatoes and they would put them in their shoes to help alleviate the biting cold of winter. My Grandpa eventually went off to learn electrical engineering on a non-combat ship in the Navy during World War II. He returned with a skill and eventually built the largest electrical contracting business in Arizona. He never received a high school diploma.

Throughout my youth, if I wanted to go shopping with him, he'd make me watch a video on smart finances or investing. He encouraged me to meditate, go on nature walks in the desert with him and my Grandma Joan and all in all, to be thoughtful and strong. Through his example I was shown mindset techniques, inspirational quotes, how to be your own boss and spirituality, among other things. These were the ways my Grandpa built his empire and looking back on my time with him, he was doing his best to instill these wisdoms into me - even if I did not live into them until much later on.

The day my Grandpa died I thought I would be able to see him and give him a kiss, as we knew he wasn't doing well. Instead, my Grandma Joan walked into the waiting room, tears streaming down her face, to let us know he was gone. It felt like a rope that I was clinging to instantly dropped off of a 600-story building and there was nothing I could do to get it back. Death can feel this way.

They let me walk into the room where he laid, alone. Looking back I am so appreciative that they gave me this space to do that even though I was so young. I had never seen anyone who had passed before. My vivacious, beautiful Gramps was gone. Head tilted back as he had taken his last breath, eyes closed, body still and cold. I walked up to him, took his hand and began to speak to him out loud through muffled tears and whispers.

"Grandpa, I am going to miss you terribly… you have shown me so much… I want you to know that I am going to make you so, so proud of me… I am going to make something big of my life… I am going to put everything you've shown me to good use, I promise…. Please watch over me as I continue on my journey… I will never forget our time together and I love you forever…"

It was a sacred experience getting to share that space with him right after his soul released the binds from his earthly form. I found myself in a deep depression for a little while, as my 15 year old life returned to normal things like school, dance and wondering how I was going to get myself into a California school when I graduated. Looking back, I have never forgotten that moment speaking to my Grandpa Mitch and I smile, because I know I have truly fulfilled my promises to him.

Fast forward from this memory and back to the moment in my car. I said out loud, "Grandpa, I wish you were here to help me with my business! There are so many questions I would ask you about being an entrepreneur, so many things I would have you clarify for me…" I spoke into the nothingness of my empty car, but into the fullness of the Universe.

About three weeks later I was on the phone with my mom, who said she had a book of my Grandpa's that she wanted to send to me. I wondered what it could be.

Sure enough, it was *Pathways to Power by Edward L. Kramer.*

A royal blue book with gold lettering. Very aged, and published in 1955. As I opened the cover, I saw my Grandpa's handwriting in it. He printed his name and address and a few quotes on the inside cover that he liked. As I flipped through the pages, I found underlines everywhere and written notes on points he felt were important. It was like getting a glimpse into his mindset on success and power as an entrepreneur, and a deeper look into his soulful spirit.

You know those moments where you're crying and laughing at the same time? This was one of those moments. I thought, holy shit, he heard me. The Universe heard me. I received what I was asking for - guidance from the man who truly started me on this path. Almost as if he was offering me this wisdom from beyond. It felt profoundly beautiful and soothing. Much of what I read in that book I have based my entire coaching and spiritual methodology around. Pathways to Power by Edward L. Kramer is like the original version of "The Secret". He shared the power of thought, how to rely on the inner mind, tools for visualization and "acting as if" to create the life you truly desire. My Grandpa was completely ahead of his time reading this kind of stuff!

What it reminds me of is this: as you build something, the disposition of your energy and your soul is truly everything. We all have our own proverbial mountains to climb in our lives and each one is unique. But where is your energy at with yourself? What is your inner dialogue saying? Do you truly know all of the power at play within you?

And as I have said before, ask and you shall receive. I asked my Grandpa for his guidance and he sent it. I could feel my soul waking up to its own power and, eventually, my willingness to authentically share myself with the world around me. We are so deeply guided and the most powerful energy is love. When you truly love someone, they are always linked to you and available to communicate with you in subtle ways, if only you ask for their guidance.

Life Lesson: Creating a powerful business, your own niche and something of note in this world requires the willingness to listen to your soul and ask for guidance often.

Mystical AF Soul Tip: Unfortunately, the book Pathways to Power by Edward L. Kramer is out of print! BUT! Here is how you can practice the main message put forth in that incredible book: practice visualization. Write down a list of 10 things that would make you SO HAPPY to experience in your life before you end your present incarnation. Then, close your eyes, center your breathing and begin to see images in your mind of those experiences in your life. Let the feelings bubble up within your body. Feel them as if they are already occurring. This is the basic premise of manifestation and what Edward L. Kramer was teaching in Pathways to Power.

Six

Pluto Transit Ascendant
Transformation Station

Pluto Transit the Ascendant: Pluto transit the Ascendant is not an aspect in the natal chart but an actual transit that is quite rare and only occurs for ONE Zodiac Sign at a time! This transit is a FULL SOUL MAKEOVER.

Planet Pluto is the energy of transformation in Astrology as well as (cosmic) death and rebirth.

This heavy-hitting planet journeyed through my 12th house of Spirituality and Subconscious Healing for most of my twenties, which I attribute to the total destruction of my old ways of thinking and being.

This period of my life ushered new, fresh and POWERFUL ways to approach myself, my life and my spirituality. The Cosmos never require that we change, but they do beckon us forward, always, in the name of progression, evolution and healing.

A quick little Astrology Lesson: in order to experience the deep, penetrating transformation of a Pluto transit across the Ascendant of a natal chart, that transit has to first begin at the very start of the 12th House.

And that's just where it began for me.

The 12th House in Astrology seems to be one of those placements that people tend to create weird stereotypes about, similar to the sign Scorpio or Gemini, or a transit like Mercury Retrograde. As I have progressed in my astrological studies, I see a lot of these stereotypes as very silly and disempowering. But as a woman who has moved through a Pluto transit in the 12th House, I can report that it is definitely very challenging, but all for the sake of self-illumination and empowerment.

So what is up with Pluto anyway? Pluto represents an energy according to Western Astrology that goes a little something like this: *TRANSFORM OR BE DRAGGED.* In other words, if you don't show up for your soul work or very simply, the challenges of your life, *LIFE WILL FEEL LIKE A DRAG!* Pluto represents our inner power, our ability to heal and transform. It's also our inner mystic, who beckons us to evolve and understand that the shadow is an integral part of the human incarnation. Everyone undergoes Pluto transits - you are having one now! Your unique Ascendant Sign determines which house Pluto is currently traversing for you, as Pluto travels through Capricorn until the year 2024.

I haven't told you much about the 12th House and I will keep that simple. If you google "12th House in Astrology" just be prepared, you will most likely find some freaky shit so I suggest you go with my definition:

12TH HOUSE - MEDITATION, THE SOUL, DEEPER KNOWING, SLOWING DOWN & GETTING QUIET, LISTENING IN A DEEPER WAY, SOUL WORK, INNER WORK, OLD STUFF YOU MUST HEAL, SUBCONSCIOUS MESSAGES & OLD PROGRAMMINGS, PAST LIFE ENERGY. PISCES/NEPTUNE RULED.

From my own experience, I now define the 12th House as this: *DISCOVER YOUR SOUL*. For anyone who has a heavy 12th House pronunciation with lots of planets and action going on in there, I see this as your soul's deep desire to understand itself while it's here on Earth.

January 26th, 2008 Pluto entered Capricorn and I was 20 years old, soon to be 21. Shortly thereafter I moved to Los Angeles, *thinking* I was to become a famous and successful jewelry designer. WRONG, says the Universe: You will be moving to Los Angeles to develop a minor cocaine and alcohol dependency, while your crippling self-doubt and low self-esteem boil to the surface of your conscious mind so you'll do the deep inner work to prepare you to step into your power as a spiritual teacher, modern mystic and women's empowerment coach.

SOUND GOOD?

The story outlined below is from a blog post I wrote two years ago, once I was finally ready to express my addictive issues and how they impacted my spiritual awakening. For many years I was pretty ashamed of this leg of my journey, simply because I treated myself with so much disrespect. This memory quite perfectly illustrates the journey of Pluto moving through my 12th House edging closer to my Ascendant over time.

October 3, 2017:

First off, I want to clear something up. Anyone, and I repeat, ANYONE can be a mystic. This is a self-given title that I have fun utilizing because I truly love the mystical components of the life journey. If you choose to study the deeper workings of the Universe and utilize the wisdom to become the most authentic and loving version of yourself, then in my opinion, you are a Mystic. Even better if you utilize those tools to help others be the best version of themselves.

I am passionate about this part of life because the Mystical saved my life.

*(*I want to share part of my old story with you here, and I hope that my expression of this old leg of my journey can assist you or someone you love move through addiction or depression of any kind.*)*

*A few years ago I was in a session with my old therapist, and I was having what could be considered a pretty massive breakthrough. I walked through my past with her: addictions of all kinds, workaholism, perfectionism, the most unhealthy relationship to my body and to life itself. I burst into tears when I remembered my turning point, of finally answering the call inside of me to get healthy and get aligned with my Spirit. This was the first moment I realized why I was so obsessed with mystical sh*t, because basically, it kept me alive and kicking on Planet Earth, instead of vacating, exiting, checking out, aka: committing suicide.*

When I was 19, I started reading spiritual books and began to study art in college. I shifted away from my Marketing/Political Science degree and surrendered to my creativity and developing a personal relationship with myself. These were some of the darkest years because so much became dislodged from my subconscious, and I had to face all of it alone, living in California away from my family. I was also wayyyy too scared to ask for any kind of help, which in hindsight, is NOT a good idea! The intensity of my emotions gave way to addiction, and truthfully, after a year of disrespecting my Being on every level, a crazy thing happened one night that changed my life forever and started me on my path with the Mystical.

Since I was young, I'd always had a strong connection to horses. My family moved to an equestrian neighborhood in Arizona and I began horse riding lessons immediately. I was a really happy kid until about age 8 when I started to get extremely self-conscious. Horseback riding and being in the desert with those sacred creatures was medicinal for me. It still is.

So fast forward many years- I found myself on a bender with my LA party crew, having heart palpitations from doing some really bad cocaine. We somehow ended up at a friend's horse stable (sounds wild I'm sure, but if you've partied before you know how those nights can go...) and there I was walking around, searching for water, dying inside.

While I wasn't physically dying, I was dying mentally, emotionally and spiritually. I finally realized I was exhausted and completely lost.

I truly hit rock bottom right there. And before I did, I stood before a stable (still in search of water), where the most majestic black horse stood. It looked back at me, caught my gaze, and whether it was the drugs or not, I literally heard something within me ask the question,

"What are you doing with your precious, sacred life?"

I felt embarrassed and small in the presence of Mother Nature and I knew that I had to change fast or I was going to ruin everything.

Why share all of this? Well number one, it is EXTREMELY vulnerable for me to share this story, not only to risk sounding slightly insane but also because no one really knows about that chapter of my life. Number two, what I learned most of all from that fated chapter is this:

ALL WAYS OF DARKNESS LEADS US BACK TO THE LIGHT.

The next morning when I woke up, I chose to forgive myself for everything I had been putting myself through and decided to make a massive change. That day was truly the first day of my journey with the mystical, and coming home into the beauty of Myself.

The mystical to me is having a deeper relationship with life and finding our self-worth and power from within. We are raised to think that everything and everyone outside of us defines our value. We have been conditioned to that idea since we were very young.

For me, journeying into the mystical gave me an anchor to explore life on my own terms. It gave me the tools to begin to define myself and most importantly, to enjoy time alone with myself as well.

If we want to find our purpose, we have to know how to be alone. We have to know how to sustain from the inside out to truly be powerful and effective with life.

I share this story in hopes that it can assist, especially anyone going through darkness of their own.

Again, all ways of darkness leads us back to the light and life is full of beauty and magic.

I never thought I would be someone who could actually say that.

x, Natalia

There it is, angels. I sound so serious in these early blog posts. Truth is, I was nervous yet ready to admit my darkest night of the soul phase. I was ready to show people who I was and how it had informed me into being a truly beautiful, powerful and soulful woman.

Eventually when Pluto began to cross my Ascendant and move into my 1st House, I PHYSICALLY transformed. People gasped that I looked like a completely different human being. The truth is, I became a completely different human being, including shifting my hair from jet black to white blonde, among other physical transformations! Throughout all those years of healing, working on myself, letting go of alcohol and partying, having two abortions, releasing disempowering relationships, and stepping into my power, I let go of some major emotional baggage. The greatest thing about a Pluto crossing the 12th House and eventually the Ascendant is this: you will not be the same person you were at the beginning, for the better. Even if this isn't happening for you in this lifetime, no worries. I have a very good feeling you still know exactly what I am talking about and I pray my sharing here gives you deep reassurance and hope that you can make it through anything.

I know that you can, because I have.

I am grateful for those dark years because they delivered me to the beautiful, strong, kind-hearted, peaceful, empowered, self-loving, self-affirming, badass, mystical babe who serves her community. Who serves more than just herself.

It feels good to be Here. Hey, thanks Pluto! (But again, thank you me!!)

Life Lesson: ALL WAYS OF DARKNESS LEADS US BACK TO THE LIGHT. Keep going!

Mystical AF Soul Tip: Want to figure out your transits? I have a gift for you, my first Course ever - MYSTIC 101 - which covers all things

Astrology, Tarot, Meditation and Essential Oils. It's my gift to you for supporting my work and making it this far in the book! In the Astrology Section there is a workbook page all about Transits, and when you learn the tool of spotting your own transits (it's simple, I promise!) it is incredibly empowering. Just go to nataliabenson.com/mysticalAF and click the MYSTIC 101 Course Tab for your free enrollment.

Seven

Mercury Conjunct Jupiter in Aries
Finding My Voice, Creating a Niche & Uncovering My Life Purpose

Mercury Conjunct Jupiter in Aries: One who is here (on Planet Earth) with the gift of GAB! Here to be an independent communicator, speak her truth, expand minds with a message, expand herself with learning. In addition, the Universe will surely show up when she is expressing herself, and most importantly, BEING Herself! Illumination via Communication!

Quick Astrology Lesson:

Mercury = communication and self-expression, aka: social media!

Jupiter = expansion, fortune, gifts, wisdom, boldness (especially when placed in the Zodiac Sign Aries!)

Aries = the sign of the independent, often expressing it's their way or the highway. A self-starter, who's willing to take risks. See: entrepreneur.

Conjunction = strong energy, almost as if the two planets in conjunction are "talking" with one another and sharing their superpowers or challenges.

It's been a long, strange and challenging journey making it to where I am now. And currently, I am writing to you from probably the most magical place I have ever been: a Mediterranean/Moroccan style Suite called the Orchard House at the Korakia Hotel, situated in the heart of a peaceful, perfect neighborhood in Palm Springs, California.

There's a saltwater waterfall/jacuzzi, and they just came around and lit the many glass Moroccan lanterns hanging from the trees. Sound magical? IT IS. I knew this would be the perfect place to channel my heart and continue writing this book. You've heard me in these last chapters express the deepest challenges of my life and I decided to share these only to encourage you that you can make it through anything and everything and truly live the life of your dreams. That's what I have done (and continue to do) and gosh darnit, does it feel amazing!

In essence, I want the remaining part of this book to be extremely useful for you and I pray all that I've already shared has served your journey. That is always my goal as a teacher and someone who is here to be so candid about her life: what can I share that helps another breathe easier, feel connected to, and thrive within the unique expression of who they are?

So let's put it this way - I haven't had anyone to "model" my career after. I've been inspired by unique teachers and movers and shakers out in the world, but as far as having someone carve a path out for me to be an Astrologer, Modern Mystic, Women's Empowerment Coach... no. Nada. In true Aries fashion I've had to carve out that hiking trail on my own, and as you can imagine from what you've read in the preceding chapters, it wasn't easy, but was remarkably worth it.

Christopher Witecki, my first true spiritual teacher you will recall from Chapter 2, was the first to point out to me: "Natalia, you are here with a message! The Universe is going to really show up for you when you share it. Your biggest message is for people to be who they are...!"

This is the easiest way for me to illustrate the Astrology placement outlined for this chapter.

March 11, 2011.

The day after the massive earthquake in Japan at Hiroshima. Major Tsunami warning, people were fearing nuclear disaster in a major way. (OK YOU WILL NEVER BELIEVE THIS. I literally wrote these words around 8:18pm PST on July 5, 2019 and then experienced AN EARTHQUAKE!.... WHAT!!! I am so shaken up but WOW how the heck powerful is that!!!!!! OK WOW, calming down soon, but wow!! That was insane!!!!)

I remember at that time feeling a growing pressure that people were going to be looking at this entire situation with so much fear and dread. I didn't 100% understand the power of vibrational frequency yet (more on that later), but the 23 year old me did have a sneaking intuition that creating something to help those around me shift their perspective around this disaster would be important.

I remembered Christopher's words, "you are here with a MESSAGE!" So, I sat down with my digital camera in my little upstairs 1920's Hollywood apartment and recorded a message of encouragement, love and hope by reciting my favorite poem from the Tao Te Ching by Lao :

> *Empty the self completely;*
> *Embrace perfect peace.*
> *The world will rise and move;*
> *Watch it return to rest.*
> *All the flourishing things will return to their source.*

This return is peaceful;
It is the flow of nature,
An eternal decay and renewal.
Accepting this brings contentment,
Ignoring this brings misery.

I probably re-read and recorded it about 10 times. I didn't like how my voice sounded, I thought I looked funny, I wasn't coming across confident or competent...the judgments were pouring through me and breaking my heart. Maybe this wasn't my "destiny" anyway! I obviously have nothing to say! (You know that judgmental inner critic, don't you?) After a few more attempts I finally slammed down the camera in contempt and shouted, "UNIVERSE, IF THIS IS PART OF MY DESTINY YOU BETTER GIVE ME A SIGN BECAUSE I AM ABOUT TO GIVE UP AND NEVER DO THIS AGAIN!" (Wow, very dramatic!) Then, one more attempt: read the poem, began with my spiritual spiel, definitely a bit exhausted from my own self-judgment and second guessing. As I began to speak the word "love" — a hummingbird flew inside my apartment. I shit you not. There it was, about 5 feet away from me. I turned the camera towards in it sheer amazement and wept. OK UNIVERSE I HEAR YOU LOUD AND CLEAR.

And here we are nearly nine years later - I heeded the sign! I now know by getting out of my own way and utilizing my voice with courage and compassion, I've assisted and empowered thousands of women. I've also built my own livelihood and niche from unleashing this cosmic, communicative superpower of mine!

You see, my entire life has opened up in the most marvelous of ways simply by being willing to express myself: even when I am scared, even when it's not perfect, even when I am not sure what I actually have to say. This is the gift of understanding your Jupiter placement. You have a unique and remarkable energy within you just waiting to be expressed! Anytime I teach about life purpose and following one's power path, I always advise people to take a look at the Sign and House placement of Jupiter. Jupiter shows where the Universe supports us, when we are willing to be bold, brave, expansive and even have fun while we're at it! I always like to say that the power and beauty we step into within ourselves isn't even about us. It's about who we are here to help and assist by shining our brightest.

So let me ask you a couple of questions. Do you feel like there is more within you that you're not sharing? Do you feel directed and purposeful in your life? Or, do you feel lost? Do you feel like you don't have a purpose? And most importantly…do you feel fulfilled by what you do in the world?

Here is the truth about purpose and why I love the magic of Natal Chart Astrology. Every Soul comes here with a mission critical purpose. If you are alive, breathing and reading these words, I am here to tell you: you are here for a reason, you simply wouldn't have been born otherwise. You wanted to be here at such a pivotal time of human evolution, at such a powerful turning point in human consciousness. You are important, you are needed and you are necessary in the unfolding of humankind's potential. And if you want to look further into your Soul's intention for your Life Purpose, take a peek at your Jupiter Placement, both the Sign and House in your Natal Chart. And if you want to get a little more advanced, book an Astrology Reading with a trusted Astrologer like the reading I had with Christopher Witecki. Ask the Astrologer to help you look at empowering aspects around your life purpose and soul's trajectory. Or, you can do what I did and keep studying Astrology, build your toolkit and learn to interpret it all for yourself. The choice is yours, my beauties.

And for you and your ever-unfolding potential: Thank you so much for showing up on Planet Earth at this time and blessing us with your gifts. We can all breathe easier and live more prosperously because you are deciding to walk the Earth impactfully, with self-empowerment, self-awareness, and love. Thank you.

Life Lesson: When you first open up your reason for being Here, it may not be easy, but that doesn't mean you should quit! Be patient with the process, love and accept yourself along the way and it's only a matter of time for the magic to unfold.

Mystical AF Soul Tip: Get a Natal Chart Reading with a trusted Astrologer. It is so enlightening and empowering. You are welcome to ask specific questions on any area of life and I absolutely suggest Natal Chart Sessions if you are pondering anything regarding your Life Purpose!

Eight

Pluto in the 10th House

Quitting Corporate & My Final Leap of Faith to Being a
Spiritual Entrepreneur

Pluto in the 10th House: intensity, drive and transformation that can sometimes feel like a small death (Pluto) Typically centers on the areas of career, vocation and higher calling (10th House). A willingness to shed old skin and embrace one's power in these realms.

Truth be told, I never completely understood this placement until later in my twenties. Throughout that seemingly fated decade I had a lot of jobs, and I mean a lot. Why? Well, being that hindsight is 20/20, I see that for many years I was very afraid of failing, just as much as I was afraid of succeeding.

So, I played small. I had a business from age 19-28 that did well but I was petrified within. Anything that truly needed to be done to help the business grow I was frightened to do because I didn't believe in myself. I had some successes, like having Tyra Banks wear some of my pieces as well as getting into Fred Segal, but none of it felt very powerful because my insecurities about myself were so disempowering. I lived off of my jewelry solely for about six years, so learn from my mistake: think of a business enterprise like a baby or a child. Would you ask your 4-6 year old to feed you? To provide for you? To pay your rent? No you wouldn't! You are meant to feed and provide for your baby, not ask it straight out of the womb to take care of you just because you don't want to get a part-time job! So needless to say, out of insecurity (as well as it simply not being my ultimate life purpose) I sunk the ship of being a jewelry designer. I let a nine year old dream die. But death is not an end. It is a transformation and a new beginning to another form of energy. As I was releasing the jewelry line, I began DJing and manifested a manager who really believed in my project. I was so ready to stop being alone all the time making jewelry in my living room-office and I felt a new energy within me brewing. I was ready for some social connection and outward expression!

Stepping out and beginning to do music was beautiful and empowering but let's just say my income plummeted. I made a pretty fast change of gears as an Aries often does, with no plan of action on the back burner. So after nine years of working for myself, I went out to get a job. I was so devoted to music and so excited at the prospect of growing my project (which was then called WHITEHORSE) that I was willing to do whatever it took to make it successful. I worked in a jewelry store and a shoe store on the same street, and hostessed at a restaurant in my neighborhood. I was also still doing Tarot and Astrology readings so you could say I was pretty dang busy!

At this time I thought music was going to be my meal ticket out of struggle, all of my Astrology and Tarot work seemed like it was there because it was my soul work, I never could have imagined it would actually be the birth of my entire career. Health and Wellness really wasn't a thing yet! It was around but still on the fringe of cool, chic and widely accepted as actually incredibly important. I illustrate all of this because you've got to just Begin Anywhere and most often times you've got to just be you and wait for the world to catch up to you. I think action is the greatest motivation and it really catalyzes change and empowerment in the direction you ultimately want to go, even if the way seems unclear. I've had so many moments in my journey where I wasn't 100% sure on where I was going but I just kept on moving, even if the movements weren't perfect. I did whatever I had to do (that was obviously moral and just!) to keep myself moving forward with what my heart felt aligned with at the time. I also didn't give a shit about people seeing me as a beginner. I think so often people don't begin on an endeavor or go for what they truly want because they are afraid of what other people will think about them.

Needless to say, I was working myself into oblivion. I'd work all day at the men's jewelry store and then go to my hostess shift at night. I'd field readings or small events on days I wasn't working. I had a DJ residence on Thursday nights and as WHITEHORSE started to pick up, I would play club shows here and there. I was teaching Yoga in my living room and reading Tarot on top of a hotel in West Hollywood on the weekends. I was so obsessed with moving forward but mostly, obsessed with not failing. I loved what I was doing but also hated it. And yet there was a fire within me and a drive that was relentless, but so often I was barely making my rent. I hadn't bought myself something new in years because it was basically pay my cell phone bill, housing costs and making sure I could eat. I knew I had to figure out what I the heck I could do to make slightly more money, with slightly less physical output. Because after a few years of working 4-7 jobs I was getting desperately disillusioned on where I was actually going and if any of it was even working anyway…

Throughout the years everyone around me kept telling me: wow, you are really good at social media! Here's another thing, back when all of this dawned on me around 2014, Social Media was NOT a job like it is now. Someone told me recently they are teaching social media at Universities, it made me feel really cute and old to be like, "WOW, they didn't have that when I was in school!"

I finally listened to everyone's promptings as a message from the Universe to help propel me forward, so I began offering social media management and consulting. Did I have any clients right off the bat? No, I didn't. But, because I was so skilled with good old SM it wasn't long before people started to message me and inquire about my services. Ironically as I began working with clients on their brand, social media expression and "content creation", it felt exactly like coaching does to me now. Why weren't they putting themselves out there with their business, music project, or the like? Exactly why I had "failed" in my earlier years: fear and lack of self-confidence to simply act and take the necessary risks to move forward. I found such satisfaction and eventually more money through teaching social media management. I did it for a boutique for a little while and eventually the jewelry store I had been working at. It was adding more to my take-home pay and to my self-confidence that my enterprising spirit was truly taking me in the right direction. And here is the thing that I learned above all else: whatever you think you are worth, is exactly what you will ask for. I teach my women now that "self worth equals net worth" because I know exactly what it feels like to not ask for enough and still scrape by. Looking back on all of this I see a theme: I was never asking for enough money because I wasn't truly aligned with what my soul was here to do. One of my favorite Kundalini Teachers Jai Dev Singh teaches that prosperity = purpose. When you are in your purpose, prosperity, money and abundance FLOWS. And I know that for certain now! I now make more in one day than I used to make it one or two months of working my 4-7 jobs. I don't say this to brag but only to illustrate that anyone can change and there is massive power in building something of value over TIME. I knew on some level I wasn't bargaining with life correctly, and that I wasn't being patient. I wasn't showing up in my full power and asking for what I was worth, and I was also expecting that somehow it would magically come together and I'd be making six figures overnight without knowing how to truly ask for it (more on that later when I hire my first Coach, Sophie…)

I think something that's commonly missing today that was absolutely missing from my own journey is true peace with the time it takes to build and create something of value. I was just so over working multiple jobs and barely making rent and would often question what was wrong with me and why it wasn't "working". It was working! Great things take time and that is okay. I think the only thing worse than never being successful is gaining success when you aren't ready for it. Success is a powerful frequency and you best be sure you match that frequency with deep self-love and respect or it could majorly fuck with your life. Success will never, ever save you, only you can do that.

Let's fast forward with another great bit of food for thought: if you allow yourself to be humble, you can learn from absolutely everything that you do. As I was building, I didn't feel like anything was beneath me: I was a personal assistant to people who were 100x more successful than me and helped them run their lives and grow their dreams. I fielded drunk dudes at the neighborhood bar and cleaned beer and wine spills off tables. I organized nearly 3 ½ years of tax receipts for someone for $14 an hour, and for a time I even managed social media for a few small technology companies. But truthfully, I learned phenomenal skills from all of it: how to blog, how to be a power house, how stressful success can be, how important a spiritual practice truly is, how to be organized, how to be humble and grateful and how to look for opportunity and growth in everything.

Now this leads me to the job that changed everything for me, which was the job I chose to finally do something for my parents. That may sound strange but I know there was a part of me that felt guilty for all of the emotions I put them through by never having a stable income or health insurance. So I took one final job for them. I also took this job because I was so scared to go it alone and do another business on my own. I thought I would "fail", so doing my spiritual work, DJ'ing (now it was called NINTH CHILD) and anything related to my soul purpose was still a part-time thing.

I took my first corporate job ever running social media for an activewear company. Needless to say after 9 months I was even more burnt out then working 7 different jobs and it became abundantly clear that the corporate life and the hour long morning commute to Vernon was not for me. When I quit I was petrified yet liberated. I knew that it was sink or swim and I was truly ready to swim. I also knew that I didn't come to this world to appease my parents and their idea about what stability and safety is, I chose to be here to be who I am no matter what. And I was finally beginning to trust myself. I had seen previous opportunities and employers so vastly underpay me for what I was offering because I didn't ask for more. I had so much experience under my belt from everything I had done I just knew the time was NOW because - when are you ever truly ready for anything? You're not! Life is all about doing your best with what you know. So I quit and then, my entire career began.

I tripled my Instagram following in a little under two years because I got so focused on writing and creating content that was of service. I started focusing on my mission, like: how can I enlighten, brighten and shine up your life on this incredible FREE social media platform? I also hired a coach, who helped me reach my six figure income within two months (more on that in Chapter 9). Basically I stopped playing small and I fucking went for it. Finally. The market and world had finally caught up to what I was embodying and I finally overcame my fear around putting myself out there. All of this has taken practice and all of this has taken TIME. But the wait and the phenomenal transformation process has all been worth it.

So Pluto, the planet of transformation and power through my 10th House of Career and Vocation perhaps makes more sense now? I underwent many incarnations to carve out my own unique niche in the Universe. If a girl from Arizona can build a successful business as a Modern Mystic and Women's Empowerment Coach in Los Angeles, and go from cleaning up beer and tax receipts to sitting at a luxury hotel in a lemon orchard writing a book about her wild, mystical journey, WHAT THE FUCK CAN'T YOU DO???

Life Lesson: Just go for it and also, be patient with the process. Success when you are not ready is worse than never becoming successful at all. And if you are willing to be authentically you and take self-guided and consistent action, it is only a matter of TIME before you are living your dream life, I promise. Begin anywhere. Start. Keep going. You fucking got this!

Mystical AF Soul Tip: FEEL THE FEAR & THE EXCITE-MENT & PLEASE GO FOR YOUR DREAMS. Write down 10 action items that would guide you to your dream life. Once you sit down and start writing you'll be amazed that you know the answers! Be willing to take action on 1 step a day, week or month. Your future powerbabe queen will thank you!

Nine

Venus in the 2nd House

Women's Empowerment

Venus in the 2nd House: Venus is our creative energy, our feminine flow and force, as well as the way we monetize or create value in our lives. The 2nd House represents productivity, money and what we value. I now teach women (represented as Venus in Astrology) how to value themselves as well as empower themselves financially & spiritually. Now, my career is the embodiment of the Venus placement in my Natal Chart.

So let me remind you this, you can do absolutely anything!! (Have I said this enough yet!?) And perhaps your Natal Chart can become a guidepost that illuminates the way for your own self actualization. Fantastically and intuitively, this is exactly what it's done for me! One thing I love about Natal Chart Astrology (and Astrology in general) is how it unfolds and evolves as you, the individual, unfolds and evolves your own consciousness. Your Natal Chart can show you the depth of your potential and all you have to do is be willing to do the inner and outer work that life offers to you. I pray that my story has done an excellent job of illustrating that you can unfold your most authentic embodiment, with your Natal Chart as a trusty guide. As I've said, if I can do it, anyone can.

It's very beautiful for me to write this chapter and really recognize the divine alignment of my Venus placement. As I outlined in Chapter 8, jumping ship from my corporate job to go full force into Coaching & being a Spiritual Teacher felt precarious yet empowering and inviting. I simply knew beyond a shadow of a doubt it was time, no matter how freaked out I was. I hired my first coach ever, Sophie, not long after quitting and it was the most money I had ever spent in my entire life. And not to mention, I had just barely started making money from coaching! I questioned myself ceaselessly: am I supposed to be doing this? Shouldn't I just keep building myself financially and figure this out on my own? Is this the right coach for me? Can I trust her? Can I trust myself? Can I even fucking do this?!

But again, something called me so profoundly to just move forward and go into the unknown. What I had learned on my own got me to the stage that I was at, but I wanted to go farther. I knew if I was going to build a foundation with my work I had to have way better pricing, way better structure and additional revenue streams other than just one-to-one coaching. I knew in my heart it was time to work with someone who was already doing what I wanted to achieve. The synchronicity of Sophie's message and her offering as a Women's Self Worth & Business Coach was just too aligned for me to overlook. She asked me all the right questions and held a steady space for me to express my power and slowly but surely trust that my mission was clear, and the time to go for it, was now.

The first session I had with Sophie, she asked me: what is your niche? What do you want to call yourself? At first that really freaked me out because committing to a single title other than Life Coach felt like quite an overwhelming task for the non-committal Aries side of my personality… The next morning I woke up early, did my morning practices, sat down at my computer, opened up the Coaching page on my website and simply wrote: Women's Empowerment Coach. I felt my heart energetically explode with gold light and iridescent glitter and that was that. Natalia Benson: Women's Empowerment Coach.

I now know that life is so much about simply realizing that you get to decide what you are, your title and how you want to present yourself to the world around you. I made up my mind to be a jewelry designer, an Astrologer, a Modern Mystic, a Kundalini Yoga Teacher, a DJ, a Life Coach and finally: A Women's Empowerment Coach. I realized for over a decade since beginning with my mystical offerings in my early twenties, I had already been empowering women simply with the language of the mystical as a buffer. I felt ready, beyond ready, to speak from my life experience of healing myself, creating businesses, failing forward, cultivating successes, branding myself, and very simply, owning my power as a conscious, sensitive yet powerful woman.

Sitting there that morning created a vantage point for me where I realized that the entire journey of my twenties had been so beyond perfect. Every mistake and challenge, every heartbreak, failure, ounce of confusion paired with the spiritual and pragmatic tools I cultivated to transform my life, created me and my entire body of work. Funny how a simple title, that feels aligned with the heart, can do that.

So once we had the title, we had to then work on how freaked out I was to ask potential clients for what I perceived to be very large amounts of money. I sat in front of the mirror and rehearsed my sales calls to myself. I witnessed how anytime I would say the price of my coaching package my voice would drop, my eyes would dart, I would almost dread this part of the call even though this was the gateway to my transformative work as a coach.

One day I was walking through the farmers market, in my head rehearsing my numbers and feeling into my insecurity around calling in new clients and selling my coaching services to them. I had just gone all in and just because I was experiencing success didn't mean I wasn't also experiencing my own self imposed blocks. I knew I was an incredible coach because my heart was all in, all I wanted to do was love, serve and guide the women who felt called to work with me. It was just the pitching and numbers that felt like this mountain that was so hard for me to run over... I said a little prayer: *Universe, I am ready for a soul mate client. I am ready to charge what I am worth. Please bring me someone who's heart is aligned with mine and we can do fantastic work together.* I then had a hunch to grab my phone out of my bag only to check my email. Just 1 minute before I had a Coaching Inquiry - someone had sent a submission form through my website. I let out a huge smile like WOW, ok that was fast! And I scheduled the call with her for the following Wednesday. Right before we jumped on our Skype call I did some mirror work and practiced speaking from my heart as I shared my pricing. I held my gaze in the mirror and reminded myself, I want to show this babe that I am here to serve her. I want to know exactly what's happening in her life and how I can be of service in assisting her to go the next level. I felt way less nervous when my focus was on service, versus myself.

When Jenn and I popped on the call together, little did I know that not only was this going to be a lifelong friendship and working relationship, but that I was meeting a dear sister and soul aligned client whom I would work with for the next year of my life.

Our intro call was seamless. We connected. She told me how she was feeling, a Pisces uninspired and quite exhausted by her current life circumstances, who deeply yearned to own her power and expand her creative career. As Jenn and I spoke I laid out a how-to plan of exactly what we would do to tackle her three main objectives during our time together. It flowed. I took a deep breath and shared my pricing. And as I let out an exhale and stayed quiet to allow her to process, she asked: "So how do I pay you the deposit and when do we get started?" Jenn would later renew working with me three times as we unfolded her power, self confidence and potential. We spoke every single Wednesday for 1 hour at a time, working through the nitty gritty details of how, when and WHY she was holding herself back from her ultimate expression of self.

I loved working with her. As Jenn and I continued throughout the year, I stepped even more deeply into my power because I never wanted to let her, or any of my other clients, down. Becoming a Women's Empowerment Coach invited me into the next level version of who I came here to be. So much of my old self-doubt, unhealthy relationships and silly bull-shit just melted away because, I was finally living my purpose. I eventually stopped drinking and I quit coffee. My nervous system was so ignited from my one-to-one sessions, I would get off of my calls and feel high. That is the power of human potential as we serve and love another. That is the power of our potential when we step into who we truly came here to be.

The most rewarding thing about coaching Jenn was watching her transform, physically, mentally, emotionally and spiritually. When we first started working together she was exhausted. Dark circles under her eyes from being out of alignment with her true self. And yes, those two things go together. When we are in the habit of telling ourselves unproductive stories those mental patterns reveal themselves through the energetics of our eyes, skin and face. As Jenn and I re-worked her old stories and kicked out shitty relationships and habits, she started to literally glow. She looked like a goddess. She got a huge raise and a bonus at work. She stood up to her boss. She kicked out anyone that wasn't in alignment with her highest, next level version of self, guys and friendships included. My Aries intensity guided her on creating boundaries in every area of her life and finally taking action on her epic creative, business ideas. We dreamed big together and we did the work. When our work together came to a close at one year it was because she was ready to rock and fucking roll. She didn't require anymore coaching, she was already starting her business (kindlycardco.com), she was dating someone really wonderful and was SO on it with her health, wellness and empowerment practices.

I felt like a proud mom. When she and I ended our last call from our one year journey together, I hung up the phone, turned on a beautiful song, danced in my living room and cried my eyes out. I didn't cry because it was over, I cried because I got to feel the beautiful and powerful force for good she and I had created together. I cried because getting to work with someone so ready to transform and create an incredible life was the greatest and most empowering feeling I had ever felt in my life. I cried because I knew in my heart Jenn and I had a karmic contract to guide one another into our power. I cried because seeing someone healed, enriched and enlivened by the same tools I utilized to change my life… indescribable.

Whenever I coach someone I transform just as much as them. The greatest part of life is living your purpose, and in my opinion the greatest part of life is when your purpose helps another soul breathe easier, heal, empower, and love the world around them.

We can all be a force for healing, justice, clarity and beauty in this world.

If I can do it, anyone can.

My Venus is placed in the sign of Pisces, in the 2nd House. Pisces is the archetype of the Empath, the sensitive soul, the creative and the spiritual guide. The 2nd House is about productivity, making money and cultivating work ethic. Not to mention the planet Venus is the essence of the feminine, of women, according to Western Astrology.

I, Natalia Benson, guide women (Venus), as a spiritual teacher (Pisces), on their empowerment, work ethic and how to build a purposeful career (2nd House). I started making money and building a phenomenal career myself when I fully stepping into my power and embodied the totality of my Venus in Pisces placement. And ironically, Jenn, one of my longest standing clients to date, is a Pisces.

I love cosmic synchronicity.

Life Lesson: Whatever you say you are, you are. So make it something magical, remarkable and empowering!

Mystical AF Soul Tip: Want to understand your feminine essence, what you value and ways to create money (honey!) in your life? Check out your Venus placement both Zodiac Sign and House!

66

Ten

Natalia's Suggested Tools

For the Aspiring, Modern Mystic & Empowered Woman

Alright my queens, well this marks the end of our journey together (for now!) I pray this book has been illuminating for you and served you and your most remarkable unfolding. As an Aries with a lot of Capricorn in my Natal Chart, I am a woman who loves practical application! I feel having the capacity to quickly implement what I've learned over the past decade has largely contributed to my success, inner peace and even my ability to write this book for you!!

So with that I give you some excellent take aways to keep your consciousness clear, your energy high, and regardless of where you are in your own sacred unfolding, a beautiful foundation to explore these practices, whether they are new or familiar to you.

Kundalini Yoga

Kundalini Yoga in my opinion is such an exquisite foundational practice for inner peace and an empowered life. Our bodies are so incredible and Kundalini Yoga really shows us at a visceral level what we are capable of feeling, achieving and embodying. My favorite teacher (and dear mentor) is Jai Dev Singh. He has an online platform called

The Life Force Academy where you can take his next level Kundalini Yoga classes from anywhere in the world! (https://teachings.jaidevsingh.com/)

Books That Have Changed My Life

Whether you love to read actual 3D books or just audiobooks (like me!) doesn't matter. Reading is so vitally important to creating a powerful life. My favorite teacher Tony Robbins says, "Leaders Are Readers!" So with that, here are some of the key books that have shaped and impacted my consciousness:

The Celestine Prophecy by James Redfield

Conversations with God by Neale Donald Walsh

Many Lives, Many Masters by Dr. Brian Weiss

Journey of Souls by Dr. Michael Newton

The Alchemist by Paolo Coehlo

Shambhala - The Sacred Path of the Warrior by Chogyam Trungpa

You are a Bad Ass at Making Money by Jen Sincero

Secrets of a Millionaire Mind by T. Harv Eker

The Only Astrology Book You'll Ever Need by Joanna Martine Woolfolk

Love, Freedom, Aloneness by Osho

Men Don't Love Women Like You by G.L. Lambert

The Universe Has Your Back by Gabby Bernstein

Mala of the Heart - Edited by Ravi Nathwani & Kate Vogt

The Science of Mind by Ernest Holmes

Red Moon - Understanding & Using the Gifts of the Menstrual Cycle

The Complete Works of Florence Shinn

The 5 Second Rule by Mel Robbins

The Power of Your Subconscious Mind by Joseph Murphy

Creating a Morning Ritual, or a Morning Practice

How do you begin your day babe? Is it rushed and crazy? Do you grab your phone first thing and scroll the Gram? If you've been with me for a little bit you know I LOVE to talk about a morning ritual. Starting your day with even just 5 minutes of inner-intention can change and uplevel your life in sensational ways! I have a really excellent formula I love to use to help you quickly and easily implement a morning ritual, even for the busiest of schedules, mamma bears included! It's not about waking up at 5am, it's about HOW you begin your morning.

Here's my Mind-Body-Soul Morning Ritual Formula:

To create your morning practice & totally change your life, choose one from each of the following Mind - Body - Soul sections and practice your ritual for 7-10 or 40 days consistently:

Mind: journal, gratitude practice, brain games, mirror work, smiling meditation, affirmations

Soul: meditation, Kundalini yoga, mirror work, breathwork, sit in silence

Body: yoga, stretching, 30 second plank, dancing, go to the gym

The No's: no phone, no self judgment, no perfectionism

The Yes's: doing your best, making the time allotment work for your schedule, consistency

Watch Your Language

No, no I am not here to scold you on not cussing (obviously!) But I'd love to check in with you on a super incredible concept I only just picked up in the last year or so: vibrational resonance and the words we speak. Our words have the capacity to make or break our energy, they either lift us up or bring us down because EVERYTHING we say, and I mean everything, our subconscious is listening to! The subconscious is the creator of your external perception of reality and it doesn't know how to take a joke. Anything you say about yourself or even someone else, it will always assume, based on word & vibration, that you are simply giving it orders on what to create and unfold in your life experience. Have you ever noticed how someone who speaks lovingly & empoweringly, tends to have a pretty epic life? Have you noticed how people who complain, gossip or speak hatefully, tend to have a pretty shitty life? This concept has nothing to do with perfection, but simply exploration, we are all human and play on both sides of the coin I just illustrated above. Here is what I'd love to offer to you: remove phrases like "I CAN'T" "I NEED" "I TRIED" "I HOPE I CAN…" anything you say after the word I especially, the subconscious goes into powerful creator mode: you say "I…" , the subconscious says "ay ay!" as if it tips its proverbial hat and takes your words verbatim as orders on what to create in your life next. So speak about yourself, and life, with empowering and loving terms. This concept takes practice but I guarantee you that as you get going with it, not only is it super f*cking fun but also unbelievably life-changing.

Consuming Mindful Media & Cultivating Empowering Activities

Your attention and focus is one of the most powerful tools that you have to create a beautiful, enjoyable life. My advice is do not pay attention to things whether it be on social media, the news or movies that hurt your heart or frighten you in any way. This is up to everyone's discretion but the truth is, wherever our focus goes energy flows. What do you want to energize and give power to in your wonderful life? Focus there. I only follow social media accounts and watch media that inspires me, enriches me and/or informs me in an empowering fashion. I am always seeking to learn and understand life from a myriad of perspectives but I make sure that the sources are coming from a place of service and education versus shock value.

Here's some of my favorite forms of media, accounts, websites and activities that enrich and inspire me on my path:

Tom Bilyeu Interviews on YouTube

Gaia TV - Yoga with Clara Roberts Oss

Natalia Benson - The App (hehe!)

Wisdom of the Oracle Deck - App

The Sweat App - for epic workouts, I love Kelsey Wells!

Pinterest: making vision boards

Making Vision Boards - IRL (in real life, too!)

Instagram - some of my favorite accounts to follow:

@iamwellandgood

@tonyrobbins

@kelseywells

@astrotwins

@ellevest

@theellenshow
@kindlycardco
EFT Tapping with Brad Yates (YouTube)
EFT Tapping with Gala Darling (YouTube)
School of Greatness Podcast - Lewis Howes
Almost 30 Podcast
Tony Robbins Events (Unleash the Power Within & Date with Destiny)

Mirror Work as a Self Love Practice

Get in front of the mirror, meet your gaze and send yourself love. Talk to yourself as if you were speaking with your dearest sister or best friend. If she was hurting you'd meet her with compassion, wisdom and a loving kick in the booty, right? Meet yourself this same way. Doing so in front of the mirror is one way for rapid transformation as well as stepping into the greatest expression of who you truly came here to be. It's super weird and often extremely emotional at first to realize that you really have only ever looked in the mirror to primp, judge or process your appearance, so rarely to meet your own soul. I recommend mirror work as a daily and weekly practice especially if you feel ready to call love into your life (aka a partnership), heal an existing relationship, release resentment, ask for a raise, up your sales game and just in general, be the boss queen of your own beautiful freakin' life. Mirror work is a trusty spiritual tool that you can truly utilize anytime you want to.

Final Words

Just thank you.

*I have no idea how many people this book will reach and it's
kind of an Aries-sort-of-ballsy move to write an autobiography
as your first book ever. I just felt so called to share my story
with the prayer that my truth, self awareness and vulnerability
could assist whoever feels called to these pages on their unique
journey towards empowerment, inner peace and purpose.
I love this life so deeply and I am grateful for the opportunity
to express myself with all of you as I do. Thank you,
thank you, thank you. This book is dedicated to you and
your sacred, unfolding. May your journey be sublime
and sweet, full of growth, love and adventure.
I look forward to seeing you soon.*

With love & deep gratitude,
Natalia Benson

Natalia Benson is a Women's Empowerment Coach, Modern Mystic & Astrologer living in Los Angeles.

Born and raised in Phoenix, Arizona Natalia has forged her own career path in LA fusing esoteric wisdom with practical modern tools in order to live a more empowered, peaceful and prosperous life.

Natalia has worked with thousands of clients and a myriad of lifestyle brands over the last decade offering her unique brand of pragmatic mysticism that encourages self awareness and an empowering outlook on life.

She encourages women to honor their astrological natal charts, feminine energy and inherent wisdom while keeping it light, relatable & inspiring.

Natalia, her pup Tarot and beautiful Capricorn boyfriend Mick, live between two wonderful Southern California cities: LA & Palm Springs. She plans to write her second book ever: A Soulful Guidebook For Women In Their Twenties and launch her second ever self empowerment coaching certification in 2021.

You can keep up with all things astrology, mysticism, empowerment & Natalia at:

nataliabenson.com & on Instagram: @natalia_benson